The Rule of Law i

Enabling students to distinguish righ

Written by Christopher Yeates

Illustrated by Zoe Sadler

Note to teachers:

The content of this book expands and elaborates on the themes presented in the Key Stage 2 series by the same author. In some places the text and accompanying illustrations from the Key Stage 2 books are reproduced here verbatim, or in very similar form.

© Gresham Books 2017
Published by Gresham Books Limited
The Carriage House, Ningwood Manor, Ningwood,
Isle of Wight PO30 4NJ
ISBN 978-0-946095-88-9

Printed in Great Britain

CONTENTS

BRITISH VALUES

Britain is made up of England, Wales and Scotland, and the people who live in these countries are called British. The people of Northern Ireland may also call themselves British and together we make up the United Kingdom. This book is to help you learn about and come to understand some of the British Values we all share.

INTRODUCTION

Critical thinking – how to read this book

In this book you will be asked to debate and evaluate situations and then decide what you think. When you debate, evaluate and decide, you are using your powers of critical thinking.

Learning to become a strong critical thinker will help you think clearly and rationally about what to believe, say, write and do.

The processes of critical thinking provide you with a series of steps to help you analyse, evaluate, debate and decide what you think about situations or choices for yourself.

Step 1: Analyse

What are the facts of the situation or choice?
How do you know the facts are true? Is there any evidence? Is the evidence trustworthy?

Step 2: Debate

Consider all points of view – especially if you disagree – and let everyone have their say. Do you have reasons to support your views? Is there evidence to support your point of view or that of others? Do you think this evidence is strong or weak?

Step 3: Keep an open mind

Are you being open-minded? Are you prepared to listen to the reasons of others and change your mind if their reasons are persuasive? Being prepared to be open-minded is an essential part of becoming a strong critical thinker.

Be honest with yourself. Check for prejudice. Are you being prejudiced? Are others being prejudiced?

Step 4: Evaluate

What are the strengths and weaknesses of the arguments behind each point of view? How strong is the evidence supporting these arguments?

Step 5: Decide

Reflecting on every point of view, and the reasons and evidence you have heard, decide what you think.

To double-check whether you have genuinely been open-minded, ask yourself:

- What is the strongest reason supporting your decision?

- What single piece of evidence helped you decide?

- What reason or piece of evidence might change your mind?

What we mean when we say...

Evaluate: identify the strengths and weaknesses.
Analyse: examine something in detail.
Evidence: facts provided to help prove something is true or false.
Prejudice: a preconceived opinion that is not based on facts or personal experience.

CHAPTER 1: PLAYING BY THE RULES

Rules, rules, rules. They're everywhere, aren't they? You probably have rules at home about homework and when you can go out at night. You definitely have rules at school about not running in the corridor and keeping quiet while the teacher is talking. There are rules to follow when you play games. Wherever you are, and whatever you are doing, you are likely to find rules that tell you what you can and cannot do.

But what are all these rules for? Why do we need them? Why can't everybody just do whatever they feel like, whenever they feel like doing it?

- Rules keep you and your things **safe**. Many schools have a rule that says you must not run in the corridors. This is to stop people racing about and bumping into each other. And how would you feel if someone took your packed lunch without asking? Not very happy, probably – but every school is likely to have firm rules about not taking other people's things without asking their permission.

- Rules make sure that everybody is treated **fairly**. Being *fair* means that everybody is treated in the same way, and understanding that everyone is as important as you are. Rules apply to everybody; there is not one rule for you and another rule for the person sitting next to you. This is because rules try to make sure that everybody gets the same opportunity to make the most of their lives and talents.

- Rules help keep things **well organised**. For example, we all like talking and laughing with our friends. But sometimes, even if you have lots to say, it is important to keep quiet and listen to what other people are saying. This is why your teachers will have a rule that says you shouldn't be talking while they are speaking to the class.

As you can see, rules exist to make your life better. It might sound a bit silly to you, but having rules actually makes things more fun. Living in a world which is safe, fair and well organised is a lot more fun than living in one which is dangerous, unfair and chaotic. If you're not convinced, think of the activities you enjoy doing. It could be football, or netball, or even a computer game. Without rules and boundaries, these games wouldn't be possible, because nobody would know how to play them, when the game was finished, or who had won.

Getting into trouble because you have broken a rule can be scary. But having consequences that matter to you because you do not follow the rules is a very important part of having rules in the first place. This is because we are all *responsible* for our own behaviour. Being responsible means that it is you, and you alone, who has control over how you treat the people around you, and how you choose to behave. It is important always to try and be as fair and respectful as you possibly can. If you are fair and respectful towards other people, it is likely they will be fair and respectful towards you.

What we mean when we say...

Responsible: being in charge of, or the cause of, something.

Fair: treating people in the same way without favouritism.

Respectful: showing politeness to other people.

Chaotic: disorganised.

Debate and evaluate:

In a group, discuss:

1   Which school rule do you think is of most benefit to pupils and explain why? What evidence can you think of to support your points of view?

2   Smoking is banned in all public places in England including cafes and restaurants. How does this rule make your lives better? What are the advantages and disadvantages of this rule? What evidence can you provide to support your ideas?

Read, research and decide:

1   Write about two rules that your teachers or parents may have told you about to help keep you safe when you use the Internet and explain how these rules help protect you. Remember to include reasons and evidence to support your ideas.

2   Think of a game or sport that you enjoy playing. Explain two or three rules that help make this game or sport more enjoyable for everyone. Give examples to support your reasons.

3   Some people say good manners – like saying please and thank you – are rules to help us consider other people's feelings. Give two examples of good manners and reasons why behaving in this way might benefit you and other people.

CHAPTER 2: RULES BEYOND THE CLASSROOM – THE LAW OF THE LAND

The rules that everybody in the whole country must obey are called *laws*, and the laws that a country has agreed to impose on all its citizens are called the *Law of the Land*. You could say that laws work very much like school rules, except laws apply to everybody, from me and you to the Prime Minister. So, at school, your teacher might tell you off if you run in the corridors, whilst in our country, people who drive their cars too fast on the road will also get into trouble. They will probably have to pay a speeding fine, or perhaps even spend some time in prison. We have laws for exactly the same reasons that we have rules.

This is Lady Justice, a Goddess whose name in Ancient Greece was Themis. She is the referee of the justice system. You will notice she is wearing a blindfold; this is to make sure the justice she provides is *objective*, or fair to everybody. Lady Justice upholds *equality* by taking no notice of who is rich or poor, young or old. In her left hand she holds balance scales, which represent the weighing of *evidence*. Rather than simply punishing people she doesn't like, or just having a guess at who is guilty, Lady Justice always uses facts, proof, and *evidence*. Finally, Lady Justice wields a sword to show the power and strength of justice.

Rules and laws make life a lot better for everybody. Having a strong and fair set of laws that benefits everybody is an important part of living in a *democracy*. In a democracy, everybody has a voice, and nobody should be treated unfairly because of who they are, where they come from or what they believe. We call this idea *equality*. Equality means that everyone should be treated in the same way. Making things as equal and as fair as possible is an extremely important part of how the law works in this country.

What we mean when we say...

Law of the Land: laws we all agree to live by so that society runs safely and smoothly. Anybody who breaks the Law of the Land is likely to be punished.

Democracy: a system where the people of a country vote for representatives to run the country.

Equality: where everyone is treated the same and enjoys the same rights and opportunities.

Objective: another word for 'fair', or 'neutral'.

Evidence: facts provided to help prove something is true or false.

Debate and evaluate:

In a group, discuss:

1 Why do you think some people break the law? What should society do to help prevent this?

2 Do you think it is right that people who break the law should be punished?

3 Lady Justice wears a blindfold to show she is being objective or fair to everyone. Why do you think this is so important?

Read, research and decide:

1 Explain what we mean by the Law of the Land.

2 Who has to obey the Law of the Land?

3 Research a list of some of the laws that you and your family obey. Explain how these laws benefit you and other people.

4 Are there any laws that you think should be changed? Can you provide reasons and any evidence to support your point of view?

CHAPTER 3: WHERE DOES RELIGIOUS LAW FIT IN?

Everyone in Britain is required to obey our country's laws, which have been made by the English Parliament, and there are no exceptions to this.

Some religions such as Judaism and Islam have their own special laws that guide members of these religions in every aspect of their lives. However, it is the British *secular* law that is the governing law. Therefore, while members of these religions may refer to their own religious law, and principles, they must still obey British laws.

Access to the British secular courts is a fundamental right of all living in Britain; all are to be treated equally before the law. Therefore the rule of law applies to everyone in Britain.

Some religions have developed their own religious community councils. These tribunals may be used by members of the particular religious community to try and resolve disputes; these might be either family or commercial disputes. The Jewish community have the Beth Din Tribunal, and the Muslim community have Sharia Councils.

A person can choose to take their dispute to their religious tribunals, but they remain free at all times to have access to British secular courts, which allows them to have the dispute determined in accordance with British legal principles. The British courts apply the principles contained in the Human Rights Act 1998 to ensure that no one appearing before the court shall suffer any discrimination by reason of gender, religion or political opinions.

Sharia principles set out a code of conduct which is referred to as Sharia law. It has been created from both the *Qur'an*, the most holy book for Muslims as the word of God, and *fatwas* – the rulings of Islamic scholars.

For Muslims, Sharia law governs every aspect of how they live their lives. Whilst the laws in Britain largely cover crime, contracts, civil relationships (like marriage) and individual rights, Sharia law covers a lot more. Its rulings are intended to help Muslims understand how to live their lives according to God's wishes. In the UK many Muslims look to Sharia law for guidance in matters to do with family law. For example, Muslims will only feel properly married if they have had their own Islamic marriage ceremony, called the nikah. But to be properly married in Britain, a Muslim must also be married in a British civil ceremony, which will ensure that their marriage is in accordance with British law, and so give those marrying rights and protection during their marriage, and in the event of the marriage breaking down.

Sharia principles can also govern how to behave in finance and business. Muslim communities have their own Sharia Councils, to which their followers can refer for assistance using Sharia principles. However the individual remains free to go to the British secular court which provides the British system of justice.

The Sharia Councils can deal with matters referred to them about family arguments or business disputes. They do not deal with criminal matters. Only the British courts can deal with criminal cases.

Some people are worried that Sharia Councils may not treat women, or some other groups fairly. The British Government respects its citizens' religious views, and allows freedom of religion for each faith to practise its own religion. However, the Government is very clear that all citizens must follow the laws of our country. In relation to disputes as to family life in particular there are concerns as to whether all parties, whether they are female, or of a different faith, obtain fair decisions from Sharia Councils.

When she was British Home Secretary, Theresa May said:

"Many British people of different faiths follow religious codes and practices, and benefit a great deal from the guidance they offer.

A number of women have reportedly been victims of what appear to be discriminatory decisions taken by Sharia Councils, and that is a significant concern. There is only one rule of law in our country, which provides rights and security for every citizen."

(quoted from www.telegraph.co.uk, May 2016)

There is still much debate going on as to how best the courts of religious communities can continue to support their own communities whilst ensuring that everyone still follows our country's rule of law.

What we mean when we say...

Secular: not connected with religious or spiritual matters.

Beth Din Tribunal: a Jewish court of law composed of three rabbinic judges, responsible for matters of Jewish religious law and the settlement of civil disputes between Jews.

Sharia Law: the religious law governing and guiding members of the Islamic faith.

The Islamic Sharia Council (ISC): a British organisation that provides legal rulings and advice to Muslims.

Qur'an: the sacred book of Islam, believed to be the word of God.

Fatwa: a ruling on a point of Islamic law provided by a recognised Islamic authority or scholar.

Nikah: a Muslim marriage.

Discriminatory: showing unfair treatment of people, especially on the grounds of age, race or sex.

Debate and evaluate:

In a group, discuss:

1 Why do you think it is necessary for there to be one rule of law in our country? Give three reasons to support your views.

2 What difficulties do you think people face when they are trying to follow both the British rule of law and guidance from their own religious faith? Can you provide any examples?

Read, research and decide:

1 Write a paragraph about Sharia law explaining how Sharia law works to serve and guide Muslims.

2 Explain how the British Government has tried to incorporate some Sharia guidance into British law. Give some examples.

3 Some people are worried that Sharia law might discriminate against women. Carrying out your own research can you find any examples where this may or might not be the case? Take care to consider reasons and evidence from more than one point of view. Using the facts and evidence from your research decide what you think.

CHAPTER 4: MEET THE JUDGES – THE JUDICIARY

When we hear the word 'justice', many of us will immediately think of scenes from TV shows and films: courtrooms with stern judges, lawyers in wigs making brilliant speeches, and suspects sitting sheepishly in the dock awaiting sentence. We're not wrong to think of these scenes; but we also need to be aware that there's a lot more to it than that.

The people who look after the law in this country are known as the *judiciary*. The main job of the judiciary is to look after the UK's *legal system* – its laws, and how these laws are interpreted and applied. The main way in which the judiciary looks after the legal system is through our law courts. The court system is run by the *judges*.

The court system is what gives judges the power to make sure that the Law of the Land works well. There are different types of court for different types of crime. There are courts for dealing with minor crimes, and courts for dealing with serious crimes. Generally, the further up the court system you go, the more serious the crime is likely to be. Right at the top of the court system is the Supreme Court of the United Kingdom. The head of the judiciary is the Lord Chief Justice. It is his or her job to make sure the court system, and the judges, are being as fair and as responsible as possible.

But what do we mean by *justice*? Justice basically means *fairness*. But what is fair has meant many different things to many different societies throughout history. In modern Britain, an important part of our justice system is the idea of *individual liberty*. This means that an individual (that's you) has a lot of *freedom* to make their own choices in life. As long as you are not breaking the *Law of the Land*, you are free to act and speak and think however you like. If you obey the law, the law will protect you and help you live your life safely and happily.

What we mean when we say...

Legal System: the set of laws of a country, and how they are interpreted, applied and enforced.

Justice: the quality of being fair and reasonable.

Judiciary: the judges who look after the country's legal system, and interpret and apply its laws. They are responsible for upholding justice.

Individual Liberty: the right to act, speak, and think as you please while still obeying the law.

Judge: an important person within the judiciary. A judge is an expert in the law, and upholds justice in the courts.

Debate and evaluate:

In a group, discuss:

1 What does justice mean to you? Can you think of any examples from home or at school where adults have made 'just (or fair) decisions'? Give reasons why you feel these decisions were 'just' (or fair).

2 Consider a situation where you feel someone made an unjust decision. Can you explain why? Remember to give reasons and try to provide evidence to support your point of view.

Read, research and decide:

1 Explain in your own words the role of the judiciary.

2 Research and write a paragraph about Individual Liberty.

3 What do you think is your most precious Individual Liberty? Give two reasons for your decision.

4 The Lord Chief Justice is a very powerful and influential individual. Using the Internet find an example of the Lord Chief Justice giving his views on an important issue for our country. Do you agree with the Lord Chief Justice's point of view? Give reasons why you do or do not agree.

CHAPTER 5: SEPARATION OF POWERS

We, the people, give our representatives a lot of power. Giving a group too much power can be a tricky thing – what happens if our representatives don't use their power wisely? Or how can we be sure that mistakes aren't made? To help protect us against these potential problems, our society is protected by a series of *checks and balances*. This means giving other groups the power to *check* the work of our representatives, and provide *balance* by giving other points of view when necessary. In the UK checks and balances are applied through the *separation of powers*, by dividing the task of the state into three big chunks.

Legislature is just a fancy word for *Parliament*, which makes the country's laws. *Executive* is another word for *Government*; the Executive uses laws to run the country. And *judiciary* means the judges who interpret and apply the laws.

Legislature. Executive. Judiciary. The most important thing to understand is what each does.

- **Legislature = Parliament = making laws**
- **Executive = Government = running the country**
- **Judiciary = the judges = interpreting and applying laws**

Can you see how the legislature, the executive and the judiciary have different responsibilities? Can you see that they each perform a special, separate job from the others? They are kept as separate as possible so that all the power isn't in the hands of just a few people. This is why it is called the *separation of powers*. All three parts overlap, but by keeping each chunk separate all three can keep a careful eye on the other two.

Your school council and your teachers will both be keeping a careful eye on the work of each other. Even though your teachers and school council are both part of your school, you can see that your school council is independent and able to speak up on your behalf if it feels something is unfair, or could be done better.

In the same way, even though the judiciary is part of the Government, it is independent of it, and is free to use its power to make up its own mind about how the law should work. We call this idea *judicial independence*.

What we mean when we say...

Legislature: another word for Parliament, which makes the country's laws. The legislature is made up of the House of Commons, the House of Lords, and our Constitutional Monarch.

Executive: another word for Government, which uses the laws made by Parliament to run the country.

The Separation of Powers: the idea that the legislature, executive and judiciary have different areas of responsibility.

Checks and Balances: spreading power around to make sure that one group does not become too powerful.

Debate and evaluate:

In a group, discuss:

1 Why is it not a good idea to give too much power to one group of people?

2 Why do you think that it is a good idea for the legislature, executive and judiciary to have different areas of responsibility? Can you support your views with any examples?

Read, research and decide:

1 Describe in your own words the roles of the:
   • Legislature   • Executive   • Judiciary

2 Explain in your own words the idea of 'checks and balances'.

3 Make a list of the strengths and weaknesses of having a system of government with 'separation of powers' where the legislature, executive and judiciary each have different areas of responsibility. Thinking about your list of strengths and weaknesses do you think this system of government is a good idea? Give reasons to support your views.

CHAPTER 6: JUDICIAL INDEPENDENCE

In a democracy, the separation of powers into the three areas of legislature, the executive and the judiciary prevents too much power being in the hands of too few individuals.

The judiciary – the judges – maintain our freedom by being completely fair and objective. Objective means only paying attention to facts and evidence and not being influenced by personal likes or dislikes. Lady Justice's blindfold helps her to be objective, because it means she can ignore people who try to influence her.

For the judiciary to be completely fair and completely objective, it is necessary for it to be independent. *Judicial independence* means that judges should be protected from people or groups who would try to control their decisions. It also means they should be protected from politicians. Politicians can influence the army, they can influence the police, but they are not allowed to influence the decisions of judges. The flip side to this is that judges are not supposed to influence politics.

Here are some more ways in which the judiciary stays independent:

- It is very difficult for a senior judge to be dismissed. For this to happen, both Houses of Parliament and the monarch have to step in. Because judges know that politicians can't just get rid of them because they don't like them, they can focus on making fair, objective decisions in the courts, even if those decisions sometimes upset politicians.

- Judges cannot be sued or *prosecuted* for anything they say or do in the course of being a judge. Again, this is to encourage them only to think about what is the most fair and just decision they can make.

What we mean when we say...

Judicial Independence: the idea that the legal system should not be influenced by Parliament or the Government.

Prosecute: to take someone to court and accuse them of a crime.

Corruption: being dishonest while in a position of authority, for example, by taking bribes.

Objective: only paying attention to facts and evidence, and not being influenced by personal likes or dislikes.

In a group, discuss:

1   Why do you think that politicians might be tempted to try and influence the judiciary? Can you provide any examples where you think this might have happened?

2   Why do you think it is important for judges not to be influenced by politicians?

Read, research and decide:

BREXIT

Brexit is an abbreviation for 'British Exit' and refers to the national referendum held on 23rd June 2016 when British citizens voted in a national referendum.

Carry out your own research on the Brexit referendum and find out:
  • How many people voted in the referendum?
  • How many people voted to stay in the European Union and how many voted to leave?
  • How did younger people tend to vote?

Towards the end of 2016 the judges and the Government disagreed about how our country should leave the European Union. Carry out your own research and decide whether you feel the judges were right to disagree with the Government.

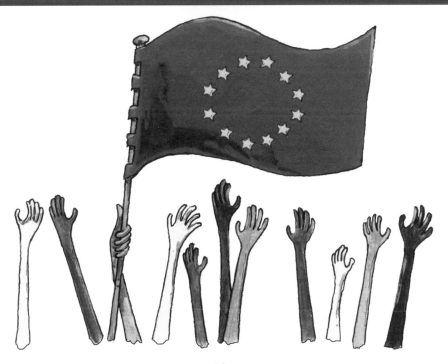

CHAPTER 7: PARLIAMENTARY SOVEREIGNTY

First and foremost, **laws come from Parliament**. This means Parliament is the supreme legal authority in the UK.

So while the judiciary is independent of the executive (Government) and the legislature (Parliament), it can only interpret and apply the laws that it is given by Parliament in the first place. The idea that Parliament is the supreme legal authority in the UK is called *Parliamentary sovereignty*. This is as it should be, given that Parliament is elected democratically by the people, and the judiciary is not.

Parliamentary sovereignty has played a very important role in the development of our democracy. Through our MPs, people like you and me have voices in how the country's laws are made, rather than powerful monarchs or an elite *aristocracy* hogging all the power. But how did we get to where we are today?

Parliament has been the supreme legal authority in the UK ever since the judges and the politicians joined forces against the monarchy in 1688 in the 'Glorious Revolution'. This was because Parliament did not like the way King James II behaved as if he were a law unto himself, and everyone more or less had to do whatever he told them to. Monarchs with complete power and the ability to make any laws they like are called *absolute monarchs*. Understandably fed up with this, Parliament invited William of Orange, from the Netherlands, to sail to England, overthrow King James, and take the throne for himself. This he duly did, along with his wife Mary. There was only one condition: to become King and Queen, William and Mary first had to agree to a very important document, called the *Bill of Rights*, in 1689. The Bill of Rights took away a lot of the monarchy's power to make laws, and gave most of that power to Parliament instead.

So ever since the Glorious Revolution it has been Parliament, not the monarch, who makes the laws everyone in the country has to obey. Never forget that first and foremost, Parliament is the supreme legal authority in the UK. This is because MPs are elected by people like you and me, and judges and monarchs are not.

What we mean when we say...

Parliamentary Sovereignty: the idea that Parliament is the supreme legal authority in the UK, because it makes the country's laws.

Aristocracy: the highest class of people in certain societies.

Absolute Monarchy: a king or queen who has unlimited political power. Absolute monarchs can make whatever laws they like, and punish anyone who disobeys them.

The Bill of Rights: an important document agreed in 1689. The Bill transferred a lot of political power from the monarchy to Parliament.

Debate and evaluate:

In a group, discuss:

1 In an absolute monarchy a king or queen has unlimited power to make whatever laws they like. What are the problems with this form of government?

2 What are the benefits of Parliament (rather than an absolute monarch) making laws? Give reasons and evidence to support your views.

3 Why is it important to use your vote in an election? Remember to support your views with evidence and examples.

Read, research and decide:

1 Explain in your own words what is meant by 'Parliamentary Sovereignty'.

2 Carry out your own research on the 1689 Bill of Rights and explain:
   • What was the 1689 Bill of Rights and why was it introduced?
   • Why do you think the Bill of Rights is so important to British history?
   • How does the 1689 Bill of Rights influence how our Government works today?

CHAPTER 8: WHERE HAS THE LAW COME FROM?

Common Law

The Law of England and Wales (English law for short) has been developed over hundreds of years and the origins of English law are older than Parliament itself.

Some laws have been around for hundreds of years, whilst new laws continue to be created to cope with new situations. For example, laws about speeding limits of 70 miles per hour would not have been needed before the invention of motor cars.

When thinking about the old laws, a useful starting point is the King's Court which was established by William the Conqueror in about 1066. Back then, the King sat on a bench in the Palace of Westminster, where he heard cases and dispensed justice. After a while, though, the King tired of listening to all those complaints so he appointed judges to decide cases on his behalf.

At that time many laws were little more than local customs, which were different in different parts of the country. So the King told the most important judges, who sat in the Royal Court at Westminster, to make laws that would apply to everyone in the same way and this became known as the common law.

Over the centuries the judges developed the common law, firstly by inventing new laws, and secondly by looking back at previous decisions in cases that were decided in the past to help them decide on new cases that came before them. This is known as *following precedent*. Important cases are recorded in Law Reports, and over the years have developed into what is known as case law. The most important point about case law is that it helps judges to apply the Law of the Land consistently and fairly.

Acts of Parliament

New laws are passed by Parliament and are known as Acts of Parliament or Statutes or Legislation.

Most new laws are proposed by the Government, although sometimes a Member of Parliament will have an idea for a new law which they hope others will support. Proposed laws are known as *Bills*. These Bills are presented to Parliament where they pass through several stages.

The initial stages occur in the House of Commons. Bills are debated by Members of Parliament (MPs) and are then considered in more detail by small committees of MPs. An MP who disagrees with anything proposed in a Bill can request amendments. The Bill and any amendments are voted on to obtain approval by a majority of the House of Commons.

The next stages occur in the House of Lords, where the Bill is subject to further scrutiny and debate.

Finally, when a Bill has been approved by both the House of Commons and the House of Lords it is passed to the monarch for final approval, known as the Royal Assent. Once a Bill has received the Royal Assent it is called an Act of Parliament and becomes part of the Law of the Land.

What we mean when we say...

Legislation: the laws put forward by a government.

Bill: a potential law that has been suggested for discussion by Parliament.

Majority: the larger number.

Debate: discussing a particular issue in detail and considering all points of view.

Speaker of the House: the person in charge of debates in the House of Commons.

Royal Assent: when the monarch gives approval for a new law.

Debate and evaluate:

In a group, discuss:

1 *'Following precedent'* means using decisions made in the past to help make decisions in the present. In what ways do you think it can be helpful to base current decisions on those made in the past?

Read, research and decide:

1 Explain the meaning of 'following precedent'.

2 Using your own words explain how we come to have common law in Britain.

3 Why do you think it is important that everyone has to follow the same laws?

Research project

The laws of our country continue to change and develop. Many years ago this country had the 'death penalty' when criminals accused of the most serious crimes, such as murder, could be sentenced to death.

Carrying out your own research find out:
- When was the last time the death penalty was used in Britain?
- For what kind of crimes did someone receive the death penalty?
- Why do you think the law changed and we no longer have the death penalty in Britain?

The Rule of Law

The rule of law is actually a series of principles or guidelines which help us tell whether the legal system is working correctly or not.

- **Accessibility:** so far as possible we should be able to know what the Law of the Land is, so that we know what we can and cannot do. For example, why do you have to go to school? Answer: because the law set out in the Education Act says that you have to. Information about the law is available publicly, for example, on the Internet. Lawyers advise people about the law and how to deal with legal problems.

- **Equality before the Law:** the Law of the Land should apply to everyone, and everyone should have protection under the Law. This means that whether you are an ordinary citizen, a celebrity or the Prime Minister, the same law applies and you should be treated in the same way.

- **Law not Discretion:** whether a person has broken the law should be decided by applying the Law of the Land, not on someone's personal opinion of what is right or wrong. This sounds obvious, but it is important. It is another way of saying that everyone should play by the same rules.

- **Exercise of Power:** officials such as judges, the police and civil servants must use their powers fairly, in good faith and without exceeding the proper limits of their powers. Everyone exercising power should be accountable to someone else.

- **Fair Trial:** everyone accused of breaking the law should have a fair trial. They should also be treated as 'innocent until proved guilty'.

- **Human Rights:** the Law of the Land should protect everyone's fundamental Human Rights. Examples include:
  - Personal freedom (liberty)
  - The right to life
  - Protection of property
  - Freedom of expression (free speech)

If all of these principles are being followed, you can be pretty sure that the rule of law is working well.

Read, research and decide:

Together in a group identify a law that appears to have been broken (for example, someone accused of robbery) and test it against each of the six principles of the the rule of law:

1 Does everyone know about the law?

2 Is this law applied in the same way for everyone?

3 Has the law been used to determine whether there has been wrongdoing?

4 Have the judges, police and any members of the Government used their powers fairly?

5 Has the person accused of breaking the law had a fair trial?

6 Do you think the law has tried to protect everyone's Human Rights?

CHAPTER 9: AN INTRODUCTION TO CRIMINAL LAW

Our country's legal system is nicely split down the middle into two halves. One half deals with *criminal law*, and the other half deals with *civil law*. In a nutshell:

- Criminal law deals with crime and punishment. Criminal law's main job is to keep us **safe**.
- Civil law sets out rules for how people should behave in society and to sort out disagreements.

When most people think of what laws do, they tend to think of people breaking laws that protect us from nasty, grisly things like robbery, murder and kidnapping. These are all criminal offences, rather than civil offences.

Sometimes, people choose to ignore the laws that are intended to benefit all of us. Criminal law keeps people like you and me safe by punishing people who break the law (commit a crime). It's pretty obvious that the less crime a society has to put up with, the happier and fairer it will be.

Prosecution and the Police

When a crime is committed, it is *investigated*. This is the job of the police. As well as trying to prevent crimes from happening in the first place, the police are also in charge of collecting *evidence* from crime scenes. Evidence is something that can be used to prove somebody's guilt in court – it might be a piece of clothing, or fingerprints. If the police find enough evidence against a *suspect* (a person that they think committed a crime), that suspect will be taken to court.

With criminal law, it is the Government, not individuals like you and me, who take people suspected of committing crimes to court. As a department of the Government, this is the job of the Crown Prosecution Service (or CPS for short). Once they have looked carefully at the evidence given to them by the police, the CPS decides whether they are going to *prosecute* the suspect. Prosecute, remember, means actually taking somebody to court and putting them on trial.

For a court to find someone guilty, they have to be absolutely 100% sure that it was the accused person who committed the crime. Suspects are 'innocent until proved guilty', not the other way round. For this reason, the CPS will only prosecute a suspect if the police have given them enough really good evidence to show that there is a strong possibility that the person might be guilty.

Criminal trials take place in courts, with lawyers, judges and juries all playing an important role in deciding whether a suspect should be *convicted* (found guilty) or *acquitted* (found not guilty). If a person is convicted (found guilty), criminal law can punish them in a number of ways:

- Imprisonment: being sent to prison. This is to punish the criminal and deter people from committing crimes in the future.
- Paying a fine: having to pay money. This might be to the victim of their crime.
- Community service: the criminal is sometimes made to do work which will benefit society.

DNA Evidence

One of the most reliable forms of *evidence* in many criminal cases is in our genes, encoded in *DNA*. *DNA evidence* can be collected from any part of us, for example, blood, hair, skin cells, and other bodily substances. It can even be used to solve crimes committed hundreds of years ago.

What we mean when we say...

Criminal Law: deals with crime and punishment. Criminal law keeps us safe.

Civil Law: sets out rules for how society is organised.

Suspect: someone who has been accused of committing a crime.

Crown Prosecution Service: the part of the Government that decides whether a suspect will be taken to court and prosecuted.

Convicted: found guilty.

Acquitted: found not guilty.

Debate and evaluate:

In a group, discuss:

1   Imagine you have been asked to investigate a robbery from a shop. Discuss in a group what kinds of evidence you think will be the most valuable to your investigation. What are the strengths or weaknesses of these different types of evidence?
   - Fingerprints   • Witness statements   • DNA evidence (for example, blood)
   - Footprints   • Tyre tracks   • Photographs or video evidence   • Documents

2   In April 2015, thieves carried out the Hatton Garden Heist which is believed to be the largest burglary in English legal history. The thieves stole over £100 million of jewels and cash from an underground safe deposit facility in London's Hatton Garden area. It is believed that the thieves got in by drilling through a wall from a lift shaft. Discuss in your group what kind of evidence you think the police collected to help identify the burglars. What would provide the strongest evidence?

Read, research and decide:

1   What is the role of the Crown Prosecution Service?

2   Explain in your own words why it is important to have evidence to help decide whether someone is guilty of a crime.

3   Why do you think that DNA evidence might prevent the wrong person being accused of a crime?

4   Carry out your own research on the Hatton Garden Heist. In the case of the Hatton Garden Heist do you think the rule of law worked well? What happened to the thieves? Do you think the thieves knew they were breaking the law? Were they caught? Did they have a fair trial? Were they sentenced?

CHAPTER 10: INTRODUCING CIVIL LAW

Civil law deals with the rights of one individual towards another and more or less everything that isn't a crime. Here are just a few examples:
- Civil law organises who owns what.
- Civil law organises who can work for whom.
- Civil law organises who can build what, and where.
- Civil law organises who can sell what, and to whom.
- Civil law organises family matters such as marriage and divorce.

Perhaps you think civil law doesn't have an awful lot to do with you yet. But have a think about this. What would happen if you went to a shop and bought a phone, but when you got home you discovered that the screen was cracked? In a world without civil law to help you, you would just have to put up with your new, broken phone. But because we have civil law to organise the rules which allow people to buy and sell things, it is perfectly within your rights to return to the shop and ask for an undamaged phone.

Have a look at the picture of the smug-looking man with the paintbrush and the woman looking rather cross. This is Michael and Jenny. What do you think is happening here? Well, the two of them are having an argument about where Michael's garden finishes and Jenny's garden starts. The fence has fallen down and Michael, who has never been very good at being fair or respectful towards others, has taken matters into his own hands and drawn his own boundary, making his garden much bigger than Jenny's. Now, this really isn't his decision to make, and isn't fair on Jenny at all. Luckily, Jenny has civil law to help her out.

Jenny cannot call the police, because Michael isn't committing a *criminal* offence by painting his own boundary. But what she can do is *sue* him. Suing someone means taking them to a civil court and trying to prove that they have wronged you. In Jenny's case, if she could prove that Michael has drawn the boundary line in the wrong place, it would mean that it would be her turn with the paintbrush, and she could draw the garden boundary line where it should have been all along.

One big difference between civil law and criminal law is who prosecutes whom. We know that in criminal cases, it is the CPS (Crown Prosecution Service) that decides whether to prosecute a suspect, based on the amount of evidence handed to them by the police. But in civil cases, it is nearly always individuals or groups of individuals who are prosecuting (or suing), not the Government. We call the person who is suing the *claimant*, and the person they are suing the *defendant*. We also say that the claimant has the *burden of proof*, which means it is up to them to prove that the defendant has wronged them.

Another big difference is that in criminal cases, the court has to be 100% sure that the suspect is guilty, or they cannot convict them. In civil cases, the court only has to decide who is more *likely* to be correct, rather than have overwhelming evidence either way.

What we mean when we say...

Sue: to begin legal proceedings against someone.
Claimant: the person who is suing somebody.
Defendant: the person being sued.
Burden of Proof: the obligation to prove something.

Debate and evaluate:

In a group, discuss:

1 In what ways do you think civil law helps protect your rights?

Read, research and decide:

1 Explain in your own words the role of civil law in Britain. What kind of problems might civil law help you resolve?

CHAPTER 11: THE COURT SYSTEM

The court system is the main way in which the judiciary is able to interpret and apply the country's laws and uphold justice. We have seen how the legal system in this country is divided into criminal law and civil law. This is exactly how the court system works, too.

The court system is a *hierarchy*. As you go higher up the court system on both the criminal side and the civil side, the cases become more and more serious, and the judges becomes more and more senior.

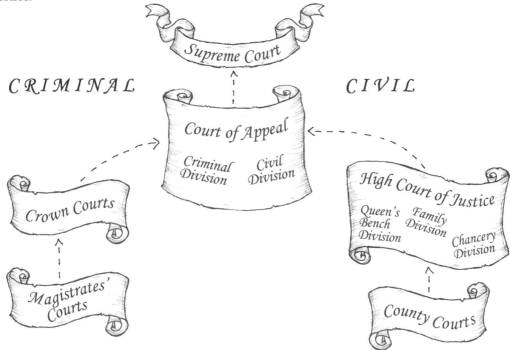

- **Magistrates' Courts:** this court deals with minor criminal offences such as driving too fast on the motorway.
- **Crown Courts:** this court deals with serious criminal offences such as murder.
- **County Courts:** this court deals with minor civil cases involving small amounts of money.
- **High Courts of Justice:** this important court is split into three sections, which each specialise in a different part of the law.
- **Court of Appeal:** this very senior court only hears very important cases, which are often important to the whole country.
- **Supreme Court:** the most important court in the UK. Every court, judge and citizen in the land must respect what the Supreme Court decides. The Supreme Court, as well as being the final court of appeal, plays an important role in the development of United Kingdom law.

The arrows you can see show how a defendant can *appeal* to a higher court. Appeals happen when a defendant thinks there might be a chance that they have been given the **wrong verdict**. Appeals in criminal cases are very rare, because as we have seen, a defendant can only be found guilty if there is overwhelming evidence against them. This makes it extremely unlikely that an innocent person is ever found guilty of a crime they did not commit.

DO YOU REMEMBER?

Let's finish by reminding ourselves of some of the most important points we've learned:

- Laws are just like the rules you have at home and at school. We have rules and laws for everyone's benefit; to help keep our lives safe, fair, and organised.

- We have a judiciary to look after the country's legal system. The judiciary is made up of judges who interpret and apply laws within the court system.

- Living under the Law of the Land protects our individual liberty, our equality, and our democracy.

- Access to the British secular courts is a fundamental right of all living in Britain, all are to be treated equally before the law.

- Muslim communities have their own Sharia Councils, to which their followers can ask for assistance using Sharia principles. However the individual remains free to go to the British secular court which provides the British system of justice.

- We use a system called Parliamentary democracy to elect MPs to represent our views and make our laws in the House of Commons.

- The separation of powers helps provide 'checks and balances' – a way of both keeping an eye on those in power, and not giving too much power to one group.

- The separation of powers can be broken down like this:
  - Legislature = Parliament = making laws
  - Executive = Government = running the country
  - Judiciary = the judges = applying and interpreting laws

- Judicial independence tries to make sure that our justice system is objective and fair.

- Parliament (the legislature) is the supreme legal authority in the UK, because it makes our country's laws. This is called Parliamentary sovereignty.

- Our justice system has developed over hundreds of years, and is still developing today.

- The Supreme Court is the most important court in the UK.